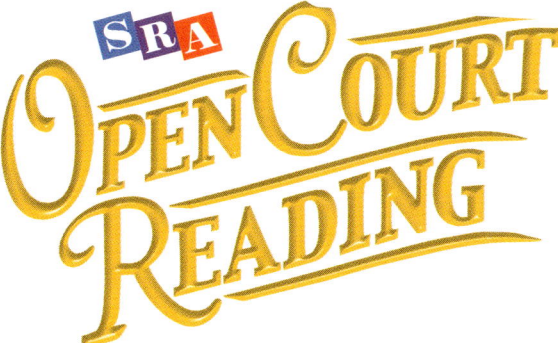

Gem Gets a Bath

A Division of The McGraw·Hill Companies

Columbus, Ohio

www.sra4kids.com

SRA/McGraw-Hill
A Division of The **McGraw·Hill** Companies

Copyright © 2002 by SRA/McGraw-Hill.

All rights reserved. Except as permitted under the United States Copyright Act, no part of this publication may be reproduced or distributed in any form or by any means, or stored in a database or retrieval system, without prior written permission from the publisher.

Printed in the United States of America.

Send all inquiries to:
SRA/McGraw-Hill
8787 Orion Place
Columbus, OH 43240-4027

ISBN 0-07-569737-8
3 4 5 6 7 8 9 DBH 05 04 03 02

Gerald has a large German shepherd named Gem.
Gem is nice and gentle.
Gem likes to run and play.

Gerald tells Gem to run and play.
Gem runs and plays.
Gem also sniffs and digs.

Look! Gem has made a mess!

Gerald sees the mess Gem has made.
Gerald must pick up the mess.

Gerald thinks he is finished,
but Gem is still a mess!
What will Gerald do with Gem?
Gerald will give Gem a bath.

Gerald rubs bath gel on Gem with a rag.
Gem is glad to have a bath.
What would Gem do without Gerald?